Minnesota's Hidden Alphabet

Minnesota's Hidden Alphabet

Photographs by **Joe Rossi** • Text by **David LaRochelle**

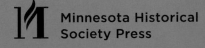 **Minnesota Historical Society Press**

www.mhspress.org

The Minnesota Historical Society Press is a member of the Association of American University Presses.

Book design by Brian Donahue/bedesign, inc.

Manufactured in China, August 2010, by Pettit Network Inc., Afton, MN

This product conforms to CPSIA 2008

10 9 8 7 6 5 4 3 2

♾ The paper used in this publication meets the minimum requirements of the American National Standard for Information Sciences—Permanence for Printed Library Materials, ANSI Z39.48-1984.

International Standard Book Number
ISBN-13: 978-0-87351-808-6 (cloth)

Library of Congress Cataloging-in-Publication Data

Rossi, Joe, 1953–
    Minnesota's hidden alphabet / photographs by Joe Rossi ; text by David LaRochelle.
      p. cm.
    ISBN 978-0-87351-808-6 (hardcover : alk. paper)
    1. Minnesota—Pictorial works—Juvenile literature. 2. Natural history—Minnesota—Pictorial works—Juvenile literature. 3. Alphabet books. I. LaRochelle, David. II. Title.
    F607.R67 2011
    977.6—dc22
            2010014997

Award-winning photographer **Joe Rossi** traveled the state in search of all the letters of the alphabet, photographing scenes from Granite Falls to Chippewa National Forest, from Bemidji to St. Paul. He lives in northern Minnesota. **David LaRochelle** is the award-winning author of *The End* and *The Best Pet of All*. He lives in White Bear Lake.

What do you see? A dead cedar tree . . . or a moss-covered letter A? If you were a bug, you might see a cozy place to lay your eggs. If you were a woodpecker, you might see the perfect spot to drill for lunch. Keep looking— who knows what else you'll see!

All across this wondrous state,
Letters A through Z await...

A a

Bb

By a brook, beside a hill,

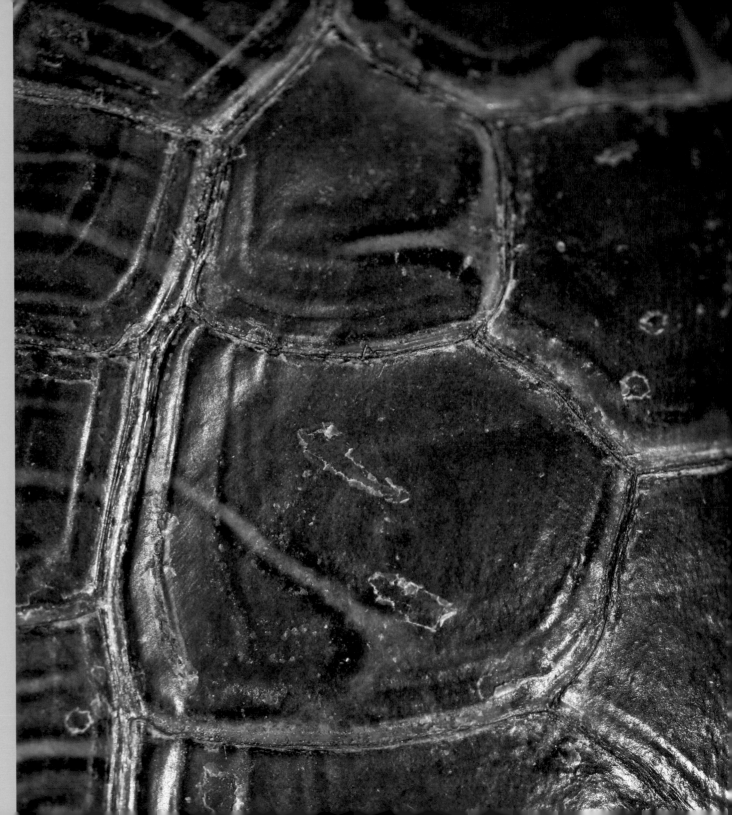

The shell of a painted turtle forms this bumpy letter B. At night when you're in bed, this turtle will be sleeping underwater, buried beneath a blanket of sand or mud. That's also where it hibernates during Minnesota's long winters, absorbing oxygen from the water through its skin.

Would you like to snack on this bony antler? Mice and squirrels do! They use their sharp teeth to nibble on antlers shed by deer. Calcium in the antlers helps hungry rodents grow their own strong bones.

Camouflaged with cunning skill.

Cc

Dd

Deftly drawn in woody glades,

You're looking down on a shelf fungus. It's growing from the side of a fallen tree and sticks out flat like a little shelf. Can you see the different rings? Every year shelf fungi add another layer, just like the rings you'd find inside a tree trunk.

You can't see it, you can't hold it, but it can knock down trees and make holes in rocks. What is it? The wind! The wind can be gentle, too. It scatters seeds, helps birds fly, and even turns this tall, grassy reed into a leafy letter E.

Even etched in blowing blades.

Ee

Ff

Found near bogs and forest floors,

Is this twig growing hair? Nope, it's just covered with a fuzzy lichen. Lichens are strange life-forms. They're made of two very different species: fungi and algae. When these two species team up, they make a brand-new, stronger species: a lichen.

Gracing gritty lakeside shores.

Does sliding around on your belly seem like an odd way to travel? Not for a snail. Snails belong to a family of animals called *gastropods,* which means "stomach foot." When in danger, a snail hides inside its shell. The shell is part of its body and grows bigger as the snail grows.

Gg

Hh

Hidden, yes, but still in view,

These bulrushes look like they're floating in the clouds, but they're really water plants growing in one of Minnesota's many lakes. In the Dakota language, the name *Minnesota* means "sky-colored water."

Jelly, flour, stuffing for life jackets . . . cattails can be made into all of these things, and more. Native Americans even used the fluffy down from cattails to pad diapers and moccasins.

I can spy them—you can too!

Ii

Jj

Jaws outstretched outline a J,

This American white pelican on the Minnesota River looks hungry for dinner. Sometimes pelicans work in a group to catch more fish. They form a half-circle and "herd" the fish into shallow water where they are easier to catch.

Waves from Lake Superior washed away the soil covering these spruce tree roots. Native Americans peeled the skin from the thin roots and used them like thread to lace together birch-bark canoes and baskets.

Kinks in roots conceal a K.

Kk

Nibbling on a milkweed leaf, this chubby caterpillar will become a monarch, the Minnesota state butterfly. Each fall, the monarchs in Minnesota migrate all the way to central Mexico, nearly two thousand miles away. Not bad for a creature that weighs less than a potato chip!

Ll

Looped on leafstalks,

This reddish-brown bark covers the trunk of a Norway pine, the official state tree. The color of the bark gives the Norway its second name: the red pine. Valued for its lumber, the Norway pine is planted by state foresters more often than any other tree in Minnesota.

Mapped on trees,

Mm

Watch out!
Mushrooms can fool you.
These red wrinkles belong
to a false morel mushroom.
The true morel, the Minnesota
state mushroom, is delicious.
But don't eat the false morel.
It is poisonous!

Notice nature's ABCs.

Nn

You'll find nests of all different sizes in Minnesota. The ruby-throated hummingbird weaves a nest about the size of your finger. The bald eagle builds a nest longer than your bed. This three-inch nest lined with soft thistledown might have been home to a goldfinch.

Overhead or on the ground,

Oo

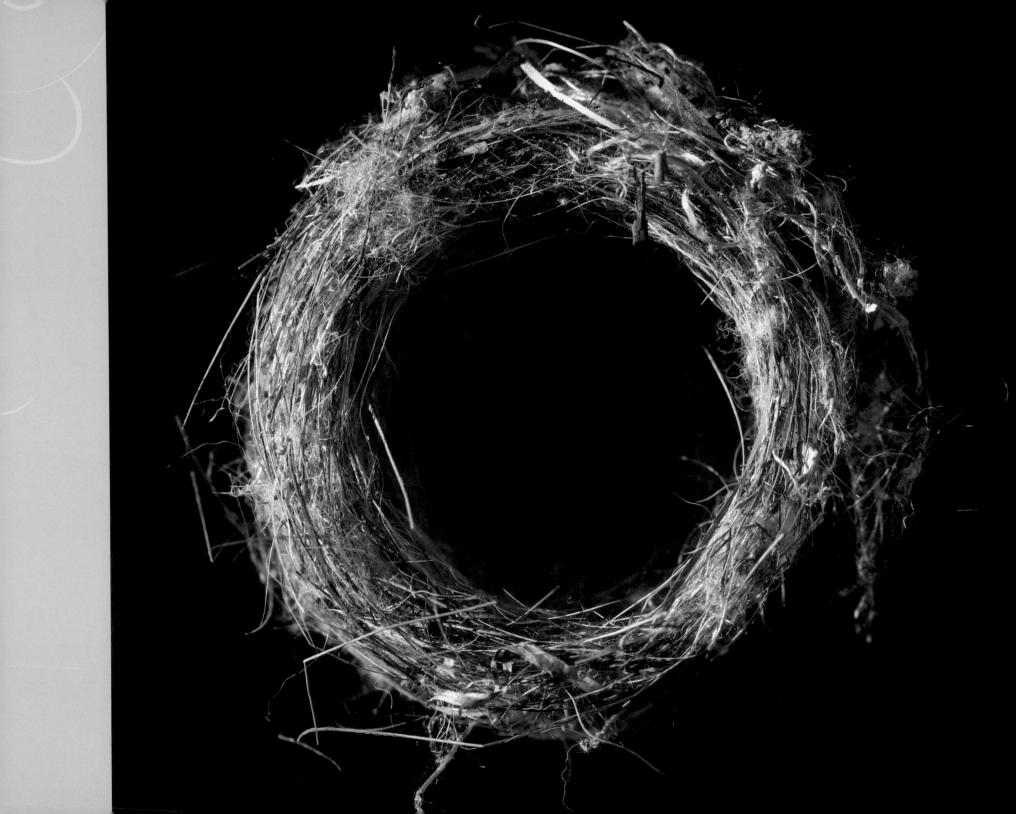

When spring arrives, look for young fiddlehead ferns like this one popping out of the damp soil. Ferns have been around for more than 300 million years. That's even before dinosaurs appeared!

Peeking, sneaking all around.

Pp

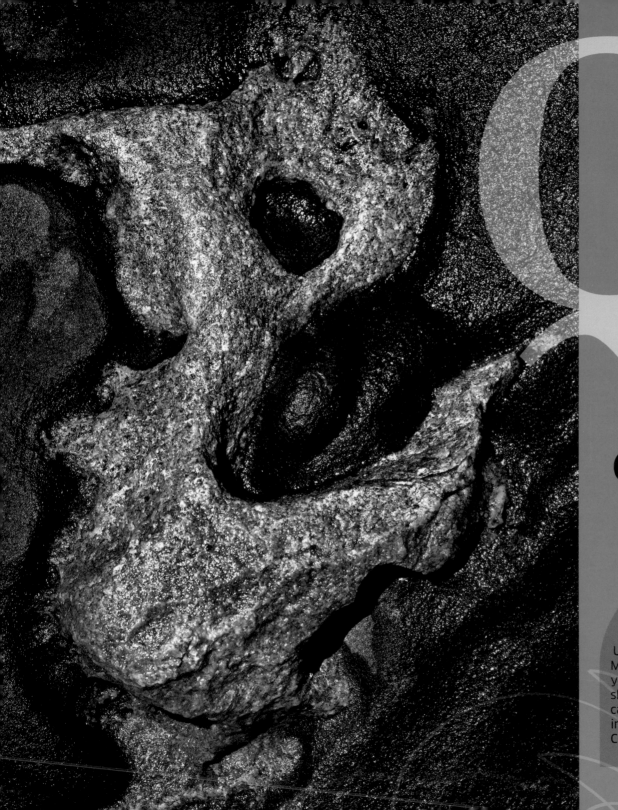

Qq

Quietly these letters lie,

Can rocks move? You bet! This lowercase q is part of a boulder from Upper Red Lake in northern Minnesota. Thousands of years ago, glaciers (large slow-moving bodies of ice) carried many of the rocks in this area south from Canada.

Ready for your roving eye.

Rr

Goat's beard, butter-and-eggs, turtlehead . . . the names of wildflowers can be as interesting as the plants. When this red blossom opens up, you'll see white puffy "feathers." Then you'll know why it's called *prairie smoke*.

Some are distant; some are near—

Ss

The tip of this bittersweet vine twists and turns like the curve of an S. Its beautiful, bright red berries appear in the fall and can be spotted even in the middle of winter, but its woody vine can kill small trees by wrapping too tightly around them.

Tt

Take your time and they'll appear.

This furry T is found on the back of an orange-barred carpet moth. Do you know how to tell a moth from a butterfly? Moths often have thicker, "hairier" bodies. When resting, moths usually lay their wings flat; butterflies fold their wings up in the air. And moths don't have the tiny knobs you'd find at the end of a butterfly's antennae.

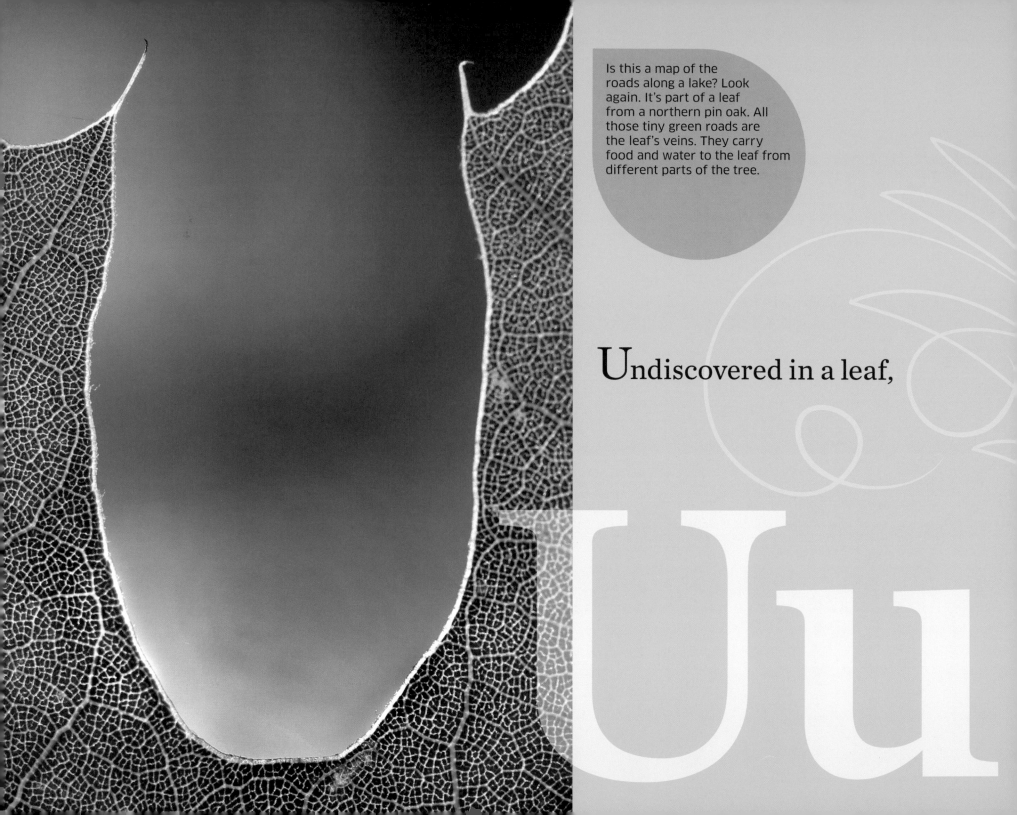

Is this a map of the roads along a lake? Look again. It's part of a leaf from a northern pin oak. All those tiny green roads are the leaf's veins. They carry food and water to the leaf from different parts of the tree.

Undiscovered in a leaf,

Uu

Vv

Velvet soft beyond belief.

Ww

Watch the woods,

Does this trout lily look like a fish? The flower might not, but if you could check its two waxy lower leaves you'd see speckles just like those on a brown trout. Also called a *fawn lily*, it's one of the first woodland flowers to bloom in the spring.

eXplore outside,

When these young wild rice plants get a little stronger, they'll stand up straight and tall in the water. Wild rice is the Minnesota state grain. The Ojibwe call it *manomin*, or "good berry." If you've ever tasted wild rice soup, you too might call it "good berry," or even "berry good"!

Yy

You'll discover where they hide.

Zz

Zig and zagging, great and grand,
Letters made by nature's hand.

What do you see?
A rock covered with
brightly colored lichens . . .
or a jagged letter Z? From
the Northwest Angle to the
southern prairies, Minnesota
is filled with hidden wonders.
Step outside and take a look.
What can *you* see?

The photographs in this book were taken in the following locations:

A Cloquet Valley State Forest
B Highway 71 between Bemidji and Turtle River
C Chippewa National Forest
D Nerstrand–Big Woods State Park
E Carlos Avery Wildlife Management Area
F Chippewa National Forest
G Rabideau Lake, Chippewa National Forest
H Rabideau Lake, Chippewa National Forest
I Carlos Avery Wildlife Management Area
J Minnesota River, Granite Falls
K Split Rock Lighthouse State Park
L Bemidji
M Preacher's Grove, Itasca State Park
N Little Johnson Lake, near Canadian border
O Macalester–Groveland neighborhood, St. Paul
P Tamarack Nature Center, White Bear Lake
Q Waskish
R Blue Mounds State Park
S Cloquet Valley State Forest
T Macalester–Groveland neighborhood, St. Paul
U Bemidji State Park
V Macalester–Groveland neighborhood, St. Paul
W Nerstrand–Big Woods State Park
X Rabideau Lake, Chippewa National Forest
Y Chippewa National Forest
Z Split Rock Lighthouse State Park